Atlantic Puffin
Little Brother of the North

Kristin Bieber Domm
Illustrated by Jeffrey C. Domm

NIMBUS
PUBLISHING

17 16 15 14   5 6 7 8

Nimbus Publishing Limited
PO Box 9166
Halifax, NS   B3K 5M8
(902) 455-4286

Printed and bound in Canada
Design: Heather Bryan
NB0637

Library and Archives Canada Cataloguing in Publication

Domm, Kristin Bieber
Atlantic puffin : little brother of the North /
Kristin Bieber Domm ; illustrated by Jeffrey C. Domm.

ISBN 1-55109-518-1

I. Domm, Jeffrey C., 1958- II. Title.

QL696.C42D65 2005   C813'.6
C2005-901970-0

Nimbus Publishing acknowledges the financial support for its publishing activities
from the Government of Canada through the Canada Book Fund (CBF) and the
Canada Council for the Arts, and from the Province of Nova Scotia through Film &
Creative Industries Nova Scotia. We are pleased to work in partnership with Film &
Creative Industries Nova Scotia to develop and promote our creative industries
for the benefit of all Nova Scotians.

Acknowledgements

One brilliant week in August, our family came face to face with Atlantic puffins on Newfoundland's spectacular Bonavista Peninsula. At Cape Bonavista and in the nearby community of Elliston we observed hundreds of puffins returning from sea with fish for their chicks. Hundreds more stood guard outside their burrow holes. When gulls chased more than thirty puffins from their island colony, the colourful seabirds sought refuge on the headland, landing just metres away from where we sat motionless with our camera gear. The inquisitiveness and beauty of these resilient creatures captivated us.

Our sincere thanks to the people who pointed us in the right direction and shared their Atlantic puffin enthusiasm and knowledge: Dave Snow of Wildland Tours, Cliff Sandeson, the Tourism Elliston Office (which hosts the annual Bird Island Puffin Festival), the Cape Bonavista Lighthouse Provincial Historic Site, and John Chardine, Marine Ecosystems Research Scientist at the Canadian Wildlife Service. Thank you also to the many students who offered important feedback during the revision process.

—Kristin & Jeff

I am an Atlantic puffin.
My scientific name,
Fratercula arctica, means
"little brother of the north."

Fishermen down at the wharf
call me a sea parrot
even though I really don't talk,
and some people say
I'm the clown of the ocean,
with my colourful beak
and unforgettable flying style.

Most of the year I live out at sea.

This isn't a problem for a seabird
who drinks salt water and has
waterproof feathers.

Every spring I return to
Newfoundland's Bonavista Peninsula,
to the tiny rock-cliff island
where I was born.

It's where I meet my mate each spring.
It's where our chick will soon hatch.

I feel snazzy in the spring when
my webbed feet and beak turn bright orange.

The added colour helps my mate and me find
each other after spending the winter apart
on the immense North Atlantic Ocean.

As soon as we see each other again we rub
and clack our beaks together to say hello.

My mate and I always find our way back
to this island, to these grass-covered rock cliffs,
to this burrow.

Many other puffins are here too,
beaks and feet busily digging nest burrows
and collecting feathers, grass, and twigs
to make soft nest linings.

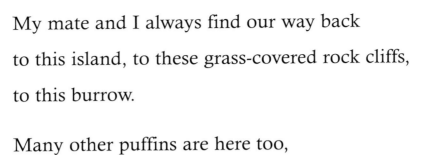

Sometimes our tunnels underground
reach back more than a metre!

Puffins lay only one egg each year.

My mate and I take turns
in the back of the burrow
keeping the egg warm.

When it's not my turn
I guard the burrow opening
or go fishing in the ocean.

Some people think I'm a fish
when they see me swim
so quickly underwater.

I propel myself forward
with my wings
and steer with my feet.

Puffins eat a lot of capelin,
herring and sand lance,
so I need to be a good swimmer
to catch all this fish.

When my chick hatches,
I will bring small fish back
to the burrow for it to eat.

Can you believe I sometimes carry
twenty fish in my beak at once?

 Today the egg is
making noise.

Our chick is pecking
its way out!

We can hear it in the quiet of our
burrow, while outside the wind is howling,
seabirds are screeching, and waves are crashing
against the island rocks.

Now that our chick has hatched
we are very busy.

Our chick doesn't resemble us yet.

He has soft, dark grey down
and big brown eyes.

After keeping the egg warm for
about forty days we'll care for this
little nestling at least another forty days,
bringing him hundreds of fish to eat
and guarding the burrow entrance.

You might think Atlantic puffins

don't have any enemies on these island cliffs,

but we do.

We keep a lookout

for the great black-backed gulls,

and herring gulls, too,

who try to snatch our chicks

or steal the food right out of our beaks!

The gulls live on our island too

and sometimes chase us away from our burrows.

Good thing they can't fit

down our burrow holes.

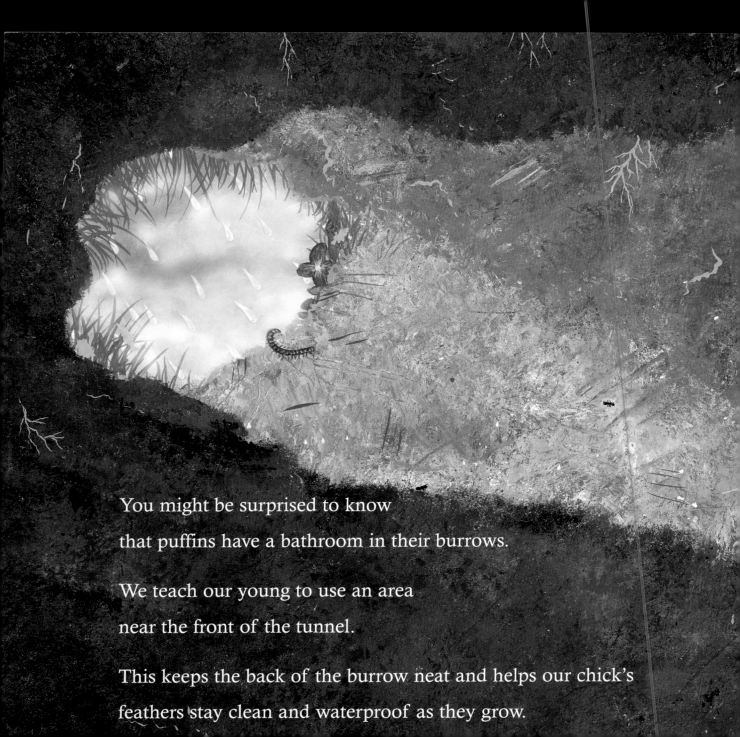

You might be surprised to know
that puffins have a bathroom in their burrows.

We teach our young to use an area
near the front of the tunnel.

This keeps the back of the burrow neat and helps our chick's
feathers stay clean and waterproof as they grow.

Hundreds of puffins
live in our island colony—
a cliff side full of burrow holes.

When we fly back from the sea
with fish for our chicks
and circle above our colony,
we know exactly which hole is ours.

Our landings are sometimes
a little rough though!

Did you know we have to flap our wings
more than three hundred times a minute
just to keep flying?

Summer is almost over.

I'm feeling the call of the open sea.

My mate and I will leave first.

Then our puffling (that's what we call him
now that he has flight feathers) will wait for night,
hop to the edge of the cliff,
and jump into the ocean.

Darkness will help protect our puffling
from his enemies as he swims away.

Our puffling will stay out at sea
for the next two or three years,
then return to these rock islands
where he'll meet other
little brothers of the north
(and sisters too!).

It's like we have a huge puffin
reunion every summer.

Aren't Atlantic puffins amazing?

More About the Atlantic Puffin

Atlantic puffins live an average of twenty years. They stand about eighteen centimetres tall and weigh about five hundred grams (roughly the size of a crow). Although males and females look alike, males are sometimes slightly larger. Atlantic puffins can fly up to eighty kilometres an hour. Their sturdy, compact bodies make graceful takeoffs and landings difficult, but they are well designed for swimming underwater. Short wings and strong wing muscles make puffins good swimmers. Their beaks are also well designed for catching and holding fish. Prompted by a keen homing instinct, Atlantic puffins usually return to the same breeding colony, the same mate and often the same burrow each year. During the breeding season, their webbed feet and beaks turn from winter grey to bright orange.

The Atlantic puffin is one of four species of puffins in the Auk (Alcidae) family of seabirds. It lives on the North Atlantic Ocean and adjoining seas, coming ashore to coastal island breeding colonies from April to August. These colonies exist on both sides of the North Atlantic and along the coasts of Greenland and Iceland.

Atlantic Puffins are often confused with penguins but the two aquatic birds are not related. Penguins live only in the southern hemisphere, while Atlantic puffins live only in the northern hemisphere. The Atlantic puffin is the official bird of the province of Newfoundland and Labrador because of the large breeding colonies there.

There are more than twelve million Atlantic puffins worldwide. (Some estimates range as high as twenty-four million.) Atlantic puffins are not endangered, but their numbers are declining in some areas. Overfishing, overhunting, fishing nets, oil spills, chemical pollutants, and rising sea levels caused by global warming threaten these resilient seabirds. Puffins are important because they teach us about the health of our oceans and how to better protect endangered seabirds.